the choice
         be-
comes
         the sign
mouth becomes

to throw
all weapons
into the cave of words

/ the speech which
turns to peace
still   every moment
but a breath, this taste
moving,
mouth to mouth
to survive.

1988

Gerry Shikatani Selected Poems and Texts | Nineteen Seventy Three -

Aya Press

Published with the assistance of the Canada Council and the Ontario Arts Council.

Cover design and concept and design of White Pine Lodge logo: Stan Shikatani Typeset in Trump and printed in an edition of 500 copies at The Coach House Press, Toronto

ACKNOWLEDGEMENTS
Financial assistance from the Ontario Arts Council and the Canada Council is gratefully acknowledged.

Gratitude is also extended to the editors of the following, for their encouragement and financial support over the years: *Aya Press; Canadian Fiction Magazine; The Canadian Forum; Coach House Press; Descant; The House of Anansi; Rampike.*

Some of these texts have appeared previously: *Cross-Canada Writers' Quarterly, Hangnail, Industrial Sabotage, Musicworks, Poetry Canada Review, SwiftCurrent, Waves.*

'end of April' is a reproduction of one example from a limited fine edition of my poem, hand-executed by jwcurry in Toronto. Kind permission to reprint is here acknowledged.

Canadian Cataloguing in Publication

Shikatani, Gerry
    1988: poems and texts 1973-1988

ISBN 0-920544-61-4

I. Title.

PS8587.H47N56 1989   C811'.54   C89-094043-6
PR9199.3.S484N56 1989

Aya Press
Box 1153, Station F
Toronto, Ontario
Canada
M4Y 2T8

To my brothers and sisters
Alan, Margaret, June, Norma, Stan
and their families;
to Kimurasan;
and to my mother Mitsuko;
for their constancy.

To bpNichol
for his extraordinary caring
and commitment to many of us.

Contents

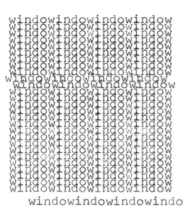

windowindowindowindow

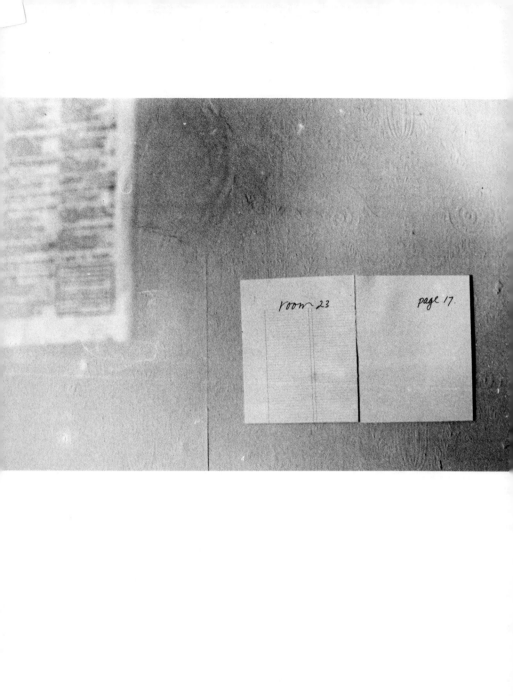

room 23   page 17.

la **una**

’l’

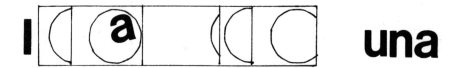

l

una

a  una

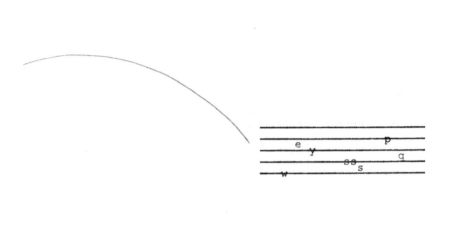

hearing of washday
I am

kitchen hides
disclosure of day's scent

under curl of lip
Japanese woman

soap, lemon, vinegar
insect sounds
in clear air

concerto music
cabaret of my mother, Mitsuko
her name

As Is

dream and moon incessant rattle
at my door, outside
strong gust and cedar
blows in front of this win-
dow.   my brothers, my sisters
who've slid me coins
through years. sometimes a bag
of potato chips sometimes
a bottle of pop. each second
figures walk past
this window elude
hand's clasp. my own brothers
sisters, you all die eventually
just dream and moon left
here. again. cedar blows
in front of this window,
the pauses and words
rattle into place.

Scattering

all a question
of reduction,   in
this flame of ideas
breathless dense
with colour.

s'
density too in the scatter:
pages in disarray
/ this desk.

I pile these pages
 together a weight compressed
into such successive
numbers: 33, 34, 36
    (35 is missing
37.
window open, voile
curtains billow towards
the desk –
this cool morning
breeze.

in a corner,
cut irises
stand on the shelf
: a ringing

of hammer and nail,
three months
ago.

Strays

Stray cats are what take flight in the mind each always. He visits almost daily then (then!) for food placed on an outside place in a plate. We didn't let him in, he came too for affection we know it, pampered once, once his old flea collar told, and we touched it. Stray came. In the flights of the mind, stray cats come and go and we are tempted to change our homes, shifters for us they meow. And then he stopped coming. He stops coming, even today. In the mind, the weapons of war burn their flights incise their light incite us to corridors of discussion. Between the action of believing in peace and hoping, there descends inevitable inaction. Reaction. Between now, the language of governments pledging their good intentions and the coming irreversible stillness there falls action which reverses intent and keeps us safe in our homes. Somewhere between such private and public, stray: it is my stray, any stray cat truly, and possibly some food scraps, surely there's enough to feed us all; and more. I saw the stray one evening, eating at garbage and I wanted this cat, possess it some more, outside myself, in an outside place there where I wanted. He does not visit anymore.

The Highway Code

1

monkey's seat   on
  the old dry birch

dropping off to the lake

2

short twig,
the lake of dead trees

3

tightly curled, hair-like
rabbit tracks,

4

fallen trees.

sunlight in soft, falling
snow –

          woodpecker chirp
past the stream
snowmobiles distant

'Are you sure?'

'Uh,'

5

to lake,
dropping off to the lake

beyond Opechee Lake

6

clearing, a single
white pine up the trail

7

slender, straight twig of buds a snow-covered
stump

8

    drops down

to lake
 fox   (prints)?

9

... hair-like
... sound of spring.

'Young

Trees

Stay

Clear'

The Strings

Voice 1:   Voice 2:

clapping
strings' edge what not at-
  centre
I'm
          at heart, the
moon, very cold
clapping against
this (oh shifting),   radii / radii
  she moves.
moon. very. cold
strings against
the edge
dancing,   'Come, come my love!'

against her will
        at heart   circum

I am at   fer, fer, fer who
she moves   fer her   cold iron
                                                      pressed to art
chill, Buddha, the still, Yahweh, Jesus, Allah,   ref, refer
                        all's circumference   fer who iron will
moon's cold   to heart
night, this breathing well,

inside
incites in
sighs the sighs, sighs the
sih sih sih
shun da shun ah uh, ih a

tonight,   a
fingernail
splits.

cold, very, cuticle. come, come,
come.

Inch Either
        Night

what moves?
               in the night
breezes
    (what
    moved?)
          crept upwards,

                                  white dresses &
                                        sandals

the fire-escape

(what moved?) ?   what? through
tree branches
light
I shifted
    in my chair,
  white   /

the breeze
summer night.

(what moved?
like vocables
      stole

speech
toward the night
in the mouth's
saliva
     (what

     going up the fire-escape
     what   in the night
     white desses
     the vocables
        toward their
    speech
what
which whisperers
like listen
to th' ears'
heart

moved
    in drastic pearl.

The Coil

cup dropped, breaks
in sink.

         this dream
lingering on empty
fingertips, painless

nearly it's dawn

One Word,

a

fragment of boulder

composition: quartz, granite

2

I'm Eastern White Pine
standing clear
in once burned
field, poplars
first to grow.
then

3

reading Shimpei's poem
   'The Desert of Japan'
finish part 4.
then

4

5.
my left hand / then
my

a forefinger & thumb
hold in air.

5

5.

sharp pain in my stomach

flames

running to toilet

pants down at ankles

sitting over the hole
for some unknown
reason it
moves in mouth,
must exit.
mumbling
'one'

excerpted from the eastern white pine
language project

if here, this
breath of pine
and be it
bare, hear
what are
its own chimes

if here, this
breeze of white pine
and be bare
October's birch
leaves gold
 in death,

if it chimes
what winds
bear
hear

breathless, a pine

dome.

51 Baldwin Street

it comes here to our back porch.

piles of fragile brown

leaves   again.

            months ago: flurries

                    then deep white days.
                    everything cold, draughty
                    silent out back.

&
again the spent leaves.
rusted, bent eavestroughs
 and filthy corners
of discarded rugs
                half-flipped over.
and the birds do return
/ the iron fire-escape
year after year.
/ the wall of gray
concrete blocks,

smell of strong chemicals
release

heaped steel drum containers.   this window
sill we painted brick red
in autumn
the cat eats the single
tender blade of new grass.

vowels carry in breeze back
  of neck cools
while the face in sun
words of the alley, gravel,
bent popcans, calls from
  schoolyard
    / spring alights here

          as everywhere
          signs – –
                  /
                the body
        .   frames
                      each   .
                thought

                    \

Heart

I

a thought travelling, also
the snow,
distance of lake,
the door closed tight.
heat moving from propane;
fingers, a nest
for words.

through this window
    / /   winter

    or distractions enough.
spots, stains
insist.
of course, unmoving
and moving!   also

        what's still and
silent I caught yesterday
in a snare.   (snowflurries:
no change forecast)
        I am in
my heart held
to my ways.   signs
cling   .

across the frozen lake
the forest slash
travel in wind,
the black ice crumbles
in a channel.

2

also.

No Thanks

nein danke
German words
I've fit in my
mouth against
nuclear power, full
of the turn on
juice, saliva, the turn
of meaning no
through hallways, even
the bare light bulb
turned out simply
the pull of
a string. lots

lots more where *words*
came from
nein danke, lots
more animal
light painted
in our caves.

In Return

What be in an open, ready mouth, bare arms outstretched from cloth, that recites with full, a roundness as harmonious spice – cardamon, myrrh; or noiseless scent, dictate with, even with hesitation. The flags, banners wave within this space enclosed, message such hallowed core so large, as is sighted land though afar, face spirited, uplifted is pressed to oncoming air: so is structure defined. This position then, King Street in Toronto at the angle it makes with Church. It is quiet (whether remembered or not, in confluence of time); it is the wooden housing of organ pipes, given to light, word-sculpted with chips hewn asunder, to polish all epistle, whether remembered or not in passing the reading hours. Pasture green, lucid under these timely arches and flags; the cathedral, day makes fragrant with hues, which studied stained glass let pass.

Who be the marching man, asks such in our place, snapping to no rules but those quick to surprise with each oncoming breath? One can image such stance: the waiter refills the cup: 'Another?' he asks with a homely order to his voice. Of course.

The banners are moving in a breeze somehow and remarkably herein. And silence walks like a cockroach, a summer beetle upon the hardwood light: always fractures. We ask for the words to commit without pause with pencil or pen.

If one's steady enough seated on the cushioned air, looking straight ahead to the curtain, the well-placed bouquet, to the fabric of such poverty-plight – there is the finger, the finger pointing with a text; and the traceable light glaze of a bowl to fit cupped palms, to hear somewhere silent a cathedral's pitched song, the platins inscribed, in the finish of housing wood.

Gathered

where this hillock
of snow
drops off –

a tangle of brush:
'spruce　　,　　Queen Anne's Lace.'

　　　　　　/

come back to where

this sentence begins.

Palmerston Boulevard

When she turns the corner, she but briefly slants chin up and outward, catching assertion, this soft feathery breeze; and she will flare memory only for days not years, but as such sanctuary from obsessive moment. With white t-shirt plain, short crop of dark hair. Her white sneakers and short socks, also white, all that is as fine. It is midafternoon: it is hot, it is humid.

When she turns the corner, she but briefly is this, a course, a trick for words to call out manifest and magnificent as a painter's brushed gold leaf. She is past and onward walking down her future, holding envelope and leather bag under arm, holding hesitations which linger in a storage of air.

Japanese Rice

Toilet paper we both hold
to ourselves to keep bed,
selves from the wet.
holding, touching myself. hold-
ing another, this other hand,
on her. the soft flesh, knee,
underside of thigh,
grasping my self, her,
at once.

My hands become wet;
the grains of rice I've
washed (circular action, cold
water and drained) steamed.
bowls of rice to satisfy,
   fill my stomach: rice, *komē*
the circle ancestral gathering
       (descendera) to self
no other, she; and I.
   wash the rice, hold myself
and her at once
with my hands. the small white
drops on my thighs
toilet paper in our hands.
we touch, cut membranes cut talk
to silence, nothing special
it's our lives,
that's it
after all.

Journal of a Trip
down to Moosonee and Moose Factory

Barrie, Ont. to North Bay, Ont.

Dunlop Street becomes Blake Street
you catch '11' going north
    exhaust fumes of bus, northbound
swing into lake,
       we sit, the wait
       flies, sunless here
    light on my woollen shirt jacket

  & on the route North
  & how Kerouac, his bop attention
has made apple pie
      taste so good, while on the
        highways

  catch '11'

in comparing train stations,
  it's this –
    Toronto's hearing muzak,
    North Bay's rock 'n' roll out of a
      sleepy transistor /
  and flies, I can't remember the
last time I saw a fly in Toronto's Union
though, it's a beautiful place, too

North Bay, Ont. to Cochrane, Ont.

been asleep and dark is lifting,
waking   shroud mist
covers the thin black rim of trees
glowing orange into blue
– mainly the pines
lifting themselves into
most prominent places
of view
amazing mist
holds these
somewhat dream states
sleep states of muskeg,
sweet mist –
lingering a
solitary barn, blackened
telephone wires, thin,
delicate, go on.

once in a while a little water
shines, a jewel,
lifting out from the gentle
roof shapes that are
as much nature, as the
mud, burrs and thick
clinging grass

a pale landscape

in water,
a rock reflects

thin green grass,
break-out water,

then slowly drifts

Notice the buildings!
   these are called mist towns
the word 'notice' re-awakens
the senses / chilled by
  morning drops
   in degrees
of air blowing,
   cushions eyelids

     the morning / like the mind/
     physicality / the body opening,

     this lightening of every
  sensory occupation, from the heavy breadth
      of sleep

  a large wide town, Matheson, Johns-Manville plant / the train
                                           blows
       slowing /   parked cars
      and gas stations,
  backs of rundown houses   roofs tarpaper

mist to a new vision of
  lakes, inlets
    trees suspended to drop-ness,

     its unreality / falsehood, as lake lies
  into mind definition is itself is
     always the extra-reality
  that is nothing more than
  reality amazing

     Amazing!
  the word
  if asked, what newness

there is, is
I would answer
  of the trees, and the water
  smoke, the sky is
  the smoke is the timber
logging, sound of saws,
smoke rising, pungent pine,
hot mess hall food
what are the names? Northern, dash, Ontario, dash
  saw-cutting splitting the sky,
    earth dank as my own
  bush, steaming cold

    you ask me to
    wake you /
        for spectacular scenery.

    but the train does move!
    quick,
        as any cricket sounds,
and as slippery / on ears and eyes,
        that you miss it
    when you look,
          reaching out from
    another heavenly sleep

        if you'd stay awhile,
you catch another glimpse
    of what is always wanted,

    but that you don't,
    sleeping by the ends,
        possessions. the dull
    of what you
        see when you
            do look
        that too it is still new,
    fast a train rolls by
of the tree
            crawling up,

the frog is croaking.

there is something about, smelling the
booze, travelling with Indians in the
train, they're rowdy & swear
    though there are straight tourists
    around / like they lack dignity
    but do not in ways to define
        that they are anti-white
            as anti-art,
                there is justice
                to this unjust drunkenness
            that travels
                    in this train coach.

I am afraid, though I respect
    their spirit skin
(the men who resemble old Japanese men)
    I can't name this fear,
that they will break out
    I will not have alibis.

dusty traintracks, stones
    all reflect the
    sunlight.

and recall Paul Radin's writing
    of the Trickster, whose pursuing
    penis, so long, was bitten off
        short, to its present length
        of who we are
        and then, these bitten became elements
        of our earth –
    and now we have harvested
    these parts, grain, water, fish,
        animals, minerals,

composed them with
scientific adhesive
synthetically, and have
re-formed the penis into
prick of porno shops
pursuing all that
exists,
we think of it as the
new coming of age, that
we hold the secrets of creation,
that we hold its roots,
that we are the
only image viable.

Cochrane, Ont. to Moosonee, Ont.

passenger-freight
to Moosonee
smell of old gray vinyl seats, chipping
paint from wooden armrests, well-used
metal, scene of cracked windows,
trains are, is this happy,
its age, children, Native Canadians, their
words that sing because this
train happy of
travelling back home,
just travelling
just a few of us
just
the sound poem that is here
child's and mother's
speech patterns
locomotive   that is
motion picture, moving
what Indian song! we board this
at Cochrane, the small northern town, it was
angle parking,
stores closed
all day Wednesdays,

at the end of Main Street, the
Ontario Northland Railway
Station.

'all aboard'   this conductor's broad grin this train their train
as this child / potato chip bag
in hand he smiles
to our hi's   that we work
with our fingers, writing,
repairing, this life we are guests,
hold the chips close, to your
young body, your eyes
and we no longer
are alone, but
joys of others who roam
hanging over chairs, to
peek-a-boo to this conductor
plays with his hat
this grin as he checks tickets, schedule book in hand,
this train's going to Moosonee,
– the luggage / what do I leave and take
in Cochrane, the town I
recorded by photograph
to dusty age from now
the coach with more and more kids
and we will disappear soon into
what is,
and that is Nirvana or some
other rock spirit, granite
the river over, moss
we are energies of dust

the karma, in, granite
we see, spectacles, glass
to see, through granite
to the, what is your
memory re-gained by
osmosis,
lamb's quarters, growing
the new seasons in
the first autumn cold.

                    more and more people
                getting on, a ringing in coach,
              Crees, watch from their small cabins,
                waving, train rolling in / like a clock
          steadily the Abitibi winding through growth, muskeg-
                flatlands of trappers' land.
                and is running to train from
          homes by the track, are running are running
                    these children! Track! rivers, streams
                rusted so red from clay, the colour
                    is Indian summer
                    like summer

Moosonee and Moose Factory Island, Ont.

                been staying   at Tidewater Park
                on Charles Island
                for last two nights /
          across   ——   Moosonee

                first night very cold, last
                    night, after a day of rain,
                strong winds, but not nearly so,
          everybody wears wool shirt-jacs,
                    wields axes, no animals yet seen
              but for the first time, tried wild plantains,
          common clover, choke cherries, which the
                    Cree, here pick
                scrubbing, charcoal   smoke stains
                from pots and pans,   at the tap
                    hands get blackish   found spruce cones
          a good abrasive cleaner, though
    scratches a bit / leaves a new smell
                    on aluminum.

                    the heavy change
                    tangle bushes,
                              worms   of older logs
                              fallen, dry or very moist,
                    ostrich ferns, pasture brake tall, inedible at this stage
          thick seasonals, scarlet fireweed, rose hips
                    light spray of verdant
                              from woody earth
                    food everywhere
                                        / poplars, alders
                              leaning away
                    from
                         Moose River,

                              click of branch against
                    moss, leaf and shoots
                         out of deadwood   greened
          to pregnancy of
                         starry shapes, arrows
                    clinging, to loosen
                         beach sand looks
     fossils
               to deserted, uninhabited
          islands, shores.

          face high, higher
                    looking up,
          dry leaves, stems full,
          we stand.

                    hail down a freighter canoe
                    man in parka
                    guides her towards
                         Moose Factory

                    beautiful isolated away
                         only trees and river,
                    lot of long-haired Cree kids,

                    staying / check-in

                              Hudson's Bay Staff House
                              150 years old.
                              very plain / you
                         hear Cree being spoken in the
                                   next room / where you are

          where are you   /   Cree spoken,

                                   a
                         working man's place,
                    dining room / for meals, well-set
                              table / ready for breakfast, help yourself
                         seconds,   thirds,
                         really stuffed.

             can see the river
                  long out as the dusk
                         sets in on Friday night
                  in Toronto you have dates
                                singles' bars,
                         Yonge Street crowd /
                         here
                              we too hung out /   overlookng
                              the Moose River,

                         is the Hudson's Bay
                  the only story in town
                  / for dry goods and groceries,
                         long line-ups
             like at Loblaws, the city's
                                   Thursday or Friday nights,

          the Cree here, eat a lot of chips,
                  and cheesies,
             we bought pop from the
                  machine, drank it
             outside the store, like the kids, the bikes around,
             watched the river
                  a small tree toad,
          our eyes amazed, the kids went

'oo oo' after it, walked the dirt roads
and even saw Moose Factory Flyers,
win a softball game, though we
got there only for the last
half-inning,
and then, strolling back,
sitting, just sitting
watching tv
at the Staff House, wordless
everything just that farther away.

and we sleep
until gray rain,
walk
between pockets of sun,
the dirt roads

back in Moosonee, the Yangtze Restaurant
(our second visit) arborite table / plastic chairs
a rock 'n' roll juke box
nothing ever different

I want coffee and french fries and gravy
'Benjamin Moore Paints' sign
and the panelling / a hangout /
Cree family out for a Saturday
stopping in /   nylon windbreakers,
the two women who helped us few days ago,
packs out of the canoe at Moose Factory,
they smile and
we are inside this Moosonee
to walk by rusty shacks, followed
by every dog
the time of our culture is
splitting

we are divided by tidewaters
that span our intentions,
towards art, made wisely
dumb
driven
by fear /   that they the Crees
know first-hand,
they smile, in shy generous ways
even in Chinese restaurants, the Yangtze
the real Moosonee,
not the tourists'
the home's inside.

by motorized freighter canoe
we cross Moose River again,
blown by wind,
high waves,   the strength
the canoe rocks,
steady yet uneasy,
we are covered with wave,
parallel action
into the channel,
safely.

winds so strong
bend everything in sight
the witchhair / dead grass
for miles, no habitation in sight
white caps, off the wind
the cold rips through clothing
to name you
you are only one man,

and across the fields, weeds
growing freely
fiercely
we are governed strictly
by what we wish
to bear

looking   out from window
flag hammers in stiff gusts:

                    side of Hudson's Bay Store
          out to
                         the dirt road
                    borders the field
          community,   lead
          out to
          James Bay

Saturday evening
no one around   but
   the evening hovers in,
speeding clouds,
the voice is what you hear
when you breathe
to live

the painting:
activity circled by
a way of life.

          walk dry snapping
          on a plain of moss:

          trees cut and burnt
               down.

          so many towns,
          tree-towns of green-ochre brown
          hillocks amongst golden hair

          breeze slips
          clearings of stars,
          animal furs,
               they are moss, such moss
               walk away

to breeze time, carpet

remarkably eternal,
   here

the muskeg –
of animal horn and antler
         years
that we cannot remember
         even when
I think, the word is
   sculpture
but it is not,
it is the source of,

we feel the wood clean
beneath bark

      breeze time

To Ship Sands Island –

   out on John's boat
      heading down to the mouth

      the big canoe is smooth
      on the Moose today.

         its rear Johnson engine
      pushes it flush,
            the red water
      to the sides

         cold, nearly freezing,
   at only the beginning of September /
      the wind makes it dip
         below

the Moose opens around
    the scarlet buoy.

    James Bay is now
    At our face!

            this wind blows without cease,
from the Arctic down through Hudson,
    and into James Bay, here at
        the mouth

            in 1611 how Hudson
                perished here / a mutiny
                    sent afloat / wintered here

    Ship Sands Island
sinking in feet out to shore,
John, Cree from Fort George,
    tells us that there is good
      ptarmigan hunting
        here

    billowing gold grasses
the thousand
    birds in
the cold pockets
dissolve,

and all land is flat.
delta, feet soaking into cold mud
        water sunken
      everywhere running out
to the Bay,
look out,

clouds build, layering
    for rain,

  a beautiful blue heron
is startled up by our
    arrival by a stream,
  flies off and wanders
we cannot come back
to where we want
    large wings what the bird,
  the span, sky sense
the wild growing, the mud, the span

  and John tells us that
the Cree couple, the only others
  on Ship Sands
  stopping off, a smoky fire
  on a log
warm, the head flies
    by smell,
           (a smoky fire
      on a log,
    by canoe with motor,
  be going up to Fort Albany,
up the Bay's shoreline, some 90 miles,

  will take 1 maybe 3 or 4 days,

    this maybe time, or as some say,
        Indian Time
  wild plants to

  fossil the current
  tidewaters bring in
  this
    history time,
    maybe the real
    wondering feeling
    the vital.

they still trap a lot in the winter, when the tourist season
dies down.

often the whole family goes up north, set lines, beaver, as
many as two hundred and fifty last winter.

The HBC (Hudson's Bay Co.);
the church, St. Thomas, white clapboard and Anglican,
    Moose Factory history
      stands, tourist spot to us,
    to the souvenir hunters,
        the instant snapshots

'a sense of our past'   Ontario history in a notebook,
    thumbnail sketch

              a white minister,
and photos of his happy
    predecessors,

        Old Testament in Cree, that is
      used /   is offered for sale, the moosehide, smoke-tanned,
      trimmed, stitched, beaded, the cloth brought faith;

        Sunday morning, evening
      they walked in the sharp wind, filed in
        to service, they are shy people
          who respect, who worship

    the sacred of place

        the medicine man
    the chief, little in evidence
    here for tourists, for us we try to reach,
    &
    hang on
    to feeling by the ends

John, from Fort George, says
that up there, trapping as way
   of life, though more fundamental
than here,
                is dying out.

Barrie, Ont. – Moosonee, Ont.: Aug. 27-28.
Moosonee and Moose Factory, Ont.: Aug 28-Sept. 3, 1974.

Shell Game

1

Coconut shells:
I remember the first time I saw a coconut
was when we were still living on Spadina.
My brother saw it at the store on College,
at the corner, and got one. And he said the
milk was wonderful inside and here we were,
it was impossible cutting through its shell,
I recollect liking its hairy texture and at
last drinking the drib-drabs of milk through the
holes, as Alan had said; and then slicing off
those crisp lush slices, the inner white meat.

2

there is a pea
under the shell.
there is a dried bean
under the shell.
there is a lentil
under the shell.
there is protein
under the shell.
our eyes are fixed

to movement. our
eyes are fixed
to movement the city
offers cool chance
the play of the street.
there are three shells
in front of us all
under each shell
there is everything.
by choice do we name
one a guess
we speak
across these lines.

Double Happiness

is a location, somewhere
nestled, at the base of the spine,
'Double Happiness Restaurant'
serving Chinese and Canadian
cuisine.

Some integer of an Asian
past, a-tumbling a translation from
Chinese, a calligram tracing
an alluring profile
finds your spine

where David Bowie is singing his
'China Girl' throwing his voice echo
out voice over the sea; the buoy
floats, red, she's racing
to the mountain, a double happiness
tied securely sash-like at the waist.

mister, please mister:
turn the page.

Like bending over, the small
of the back exposes, where
fans out the fine
skeleton of a fish. 'Fish-bone
double happiness.'

He is eating the catch, nets drawn out,
fisherman of the hand and eye:
the noble art.
It is this, caught on a hookwind
of the moon, over the urchin sea,

     Salvador Dali
in failing health, in des-
pondent seculsion since the death
of his wife Gala. 'Gala!'
Double Happiness,
rooted connection, the spine
moving the mouth with a wishbone
of the hand.

Conditions: report

pass Marten River:

check snow conditions,
what road leads down to
O-Pee-Chee Camp?
how much snow cover?

Spring-like?

can't snowshoe over
frozen river mouths,

            Ice unsafe?

check the conditions
each sign
the words

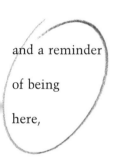
and a reminder

of being

here,

         'Groceries   Gas   Bait'
along the road, periphery
to sight, name
of camp, name
of lake, where you aim
the turn off,
    the   signs.

After Jaccottet

I

'this dream,
very beautiful, when I woke up,
coherent.'

or too is it this
French, this something language, a bit
too quick on the radio fills me
a between,
understanding a whole,
    yes, I get it.

    All which holds, centre
again September: the rain, you've
come back with charm, with
gray, I like even your hat; is it
new?

    so usual –
as household furniture
placed so, our days,

    September.

2

all colours every
where I look here
and there
fragments, new paths.

each page or card a different
hue, shuffle and flush,   or a baby's rattle

my friends who are poets
those who aren't
equally voiced, that delightful rattle!

arrange so, Gerry-o, witness

the ruffled rainbow
in this passing flight.

3

'The rain in Spain
on the plain'
'rain on the flames' (Jaccottet)
speaking of autumn
the colours, again
I return to September
rain how I return
to the world, 'fall' flaming
to hold the cold bones
assemble the chapters
the drying leaves, pressed
so carefully studied,
even loved.

Another sultry summer's passed.

The March

time marches on
bullshit,
shit what's
wretched from gut
a haunt to this
self, crouched over
toilet coughing
up, tongue's tricks.

time marches on / no
way to turn
the volatile self
from the shit bull
shit: weapons, words
on nose-cones never
stop, image
persistent the brown
coffee stain is always
on a washed teaspoon; the
ring. mine.
time marches on, its
indelible mark its work
shit, bullshit my words
or thoughts empty of force,
this satyagraha, patient
two-sided one haunts
the heart unrelenting.
a wretch
-ing to tongue
this page! a langue
-age self-defeating against

ceaseless
violent
acts. use and no-
use; function and no-
function. fuck. syno-
nym and vio
lence. a war
general and us.

Silo

my heart's aim
is that arrow

which she takes
from her mouth
and calls
'which she takes'

my heart's aim
is that arrow

showing the way;
into her plucked
from the house
of breath

my heart's aim
is that arrow

the wound exact
and sweet too
excites;
dolorous cavity and
yet our dull
principles we persist
excusing more deeply to-
gether, into night's
missing word.

my heart's aim
is that arrow
enough said:
is cliché
a half-mystery of want,
of spoken
enough

my heart's aim
is that arrow

which she takes
from her mouth
and calls
'her.'

Real Sushi

1 & 2 *Sashimi tō Maki*

Boy a lot of people,
go to bars
Fridays
after work.   night, eh?
myself, give me a bar
where knives tingle
like broken plate glass
and the refrigeration units
are clean at the bar.
not, mind you, wrists
of cool blood or the sharp
incision 'cross the cleaned
toro's stomach; but still you
hear ol' death chiming
at your door.

this is where you'd
expect I'd introduce
the raw fish
but I won't.
                    olé! olé!
                    'Eat wisely, eat fresh,
                    the rice beneath ol' death.' And

ol' death
wrapped neatly, tightly
like a thumb, with

black *nori* seaweed
a touch moistened
to secure::which doesn't
fall apart. at   the   (the faded)
the moment of contact.
Hot and Cold breeze.
whiff whiff the fan.
this holds the season's

salmon run to sea, fat
in the perch
of your hand.

3 *Nigiri*

            q

                        m

a niggling complaint,
    'so quick, this life.'

                        oh / a hold
with pressure exact
squeeze grains of rice living
bright
customers
on stools
await but
briefly,

this universe

4 Chirashi

q

m

a

a

x

a

For Gardener Poets

1

digging, turning, man-
oeuvring the soil
in a limited en-
closure.

2

what you plan and want
what you plan and don't
what you don't plan and want
what you don't plan and don't
what you don't and do
what you don't and don't

3

what you turn up,
                    (look up)

sun's spots
a paradise of eye
turns up. you turn
the log over
revealing its weapons,
a scramble of wood lice
to reveal the mind,
a charge disarming
the garden's war.

4

A charmed linkage, my friend
to take the path, string
of your words.
Each link made here to your world
'tends as bracelet to these arms,
now into such whorl we come.

5 after Robert Louis Stevenson

a limited enclosure
time to cut the grass:
time to water the lawn.
where we bring pen
to eye, eye to paper
enclosing limits.

a garden fence,
a bordering hedge,
a track of gravel,
a pile of stones,
a path of wood chips,
a running furrow
and here, not
as in listen,
we have the poet, he
is in his garden
he is eating fresh boiled
courgettes, he is savouring
new potatoes with mint, hear
as in listen, the poet
lies buried 'neath
the coverlet of leaves dry
and damp, attendant
in this garden
of verse.

large red

Specifically, My Cat

On this day, the keel is right, if it is bright. The first deep blood rouge buds have pushed forth to a sky now so blue, cleared of clouds, a new look. One reads in this a fashion text. And too, it's the same on the cement gray walk: the dots, fallen rouge pattern orders of sweep clean, sweep clean, demands in fashion, new look follows new look, winter to spring.

April, warm and sunny – baseballs reach first air, 'It's April,' we exclaim, turning our faces with the march of the sun. Yet, April too rainy with broken wind-bent umbrellas and even, yes the occasions of snow, signs of when to sow first seeds, packages shed-stored and predicting the summer. This much is known: Nothing. Or when? Certainly. The cat – my cat, specifically – eats grass and rolls about, a fat form one matches to a wrought iron fence; for both have black.

In this, the rent is to still construct the pretty colours and dark of life's old institute, a school of reminders. Dig the myths. Call up a good friend, family; call up distastes – precisely and most of all, enemies. And so the tune comes from a porch a living, five doors down the street, south, to the right: 'tis nothing of style or educated will, but a power saw's pitched yowl, the scent of wood, yes, but fibreglass most persistent, in the ordinary travel of the baseball sun.

Tea-House

everything falls away
to the edge
nothing is repeated.

each moment,
/ a woman, finely-dressed,
  work perhaps,
  walks by

/ a pigeon floats past a blue
  parked car

breathless, a centre

where words gather,
every clever perception
falls away:
the centre is breathless

like brilliant light
crescent moon
fills the pool,

heart, pure and clear
is a paradise land.

On An Afternoon

what I hurled was a descent of sparrows
a foraged pocket of words kept gloomy in
the mouth with a single green tooth. it was the plain
truth of newspaper contraction, 'life is a short patter before
the mongolling of death,' a curious traffic of words across
accident-tending city streets, long breaths of literate
                                        exhaltation
reducing of being
from tangled thought's
strands feeling, breath
and line a
memory of touch
stone cancel
'd breath
to

(the 2nd part)

Speech

2

into the breach of time
and word, habit of speech.
feeling   /   mouth.

canker sore.
in the mouth.
tongue explores the pain, through
which we see. or tastes divine
of sautéed food and wine stick
in mouth, feeling, this long
measure's reach, a prisoner's
parole. Parole is what we are
what happens at the end of speech.

it's actually falling, like from that
previous line, word.
each passing word, hurls out
the guilt of what time
it is.

3

I don't care about its ease.
movement of words, making a
play for the Big One. or her. aw,
fuck, shit, aw shit I can't write
anymore, hearing resonance of bumbling
images trapped like pillow
words. no longer knowing the exact
feelings: about love,
about image or right action,
compassion. fuck it. or some other
teloscopic.

here, standing. parked cars. parked.
cars. there's no way
around. no way
around
them.

Essay
for Lola Lemire Tostevin

All we are saying.
Is: to be
that. no not
that
the pronoun
impersonal.
non-person.
to be: essere
the Latin:
essayer to be
French. or try
to be. that.
no not that
but those. no not
those but all
of the
particular
verb which call-
i
-graphs active
and passive
/ transitive and
in, it not
the noun but
the naming,
to be creaturely
a verb,
is all we are

saying

is: present indicative
of be:

A Path Asked

breath

    & a

  stone

path

   her breath

   p

path a stony

        curve

           she

     asks.

in the air,
clear,

  clear
  a poem

   without   polluting

  yes   she
  asks   less.

A Turn of the Wrist

the smile lasts
for miles. the
horizon,
almost
imperceptible –

   crocus bulbs are sub-
merged, just
below, in the darkness
of soil –

but not

these as
'the given'
that sense of things,
but

that things to
us
attend, dextrous

unravelling
action.

With Kimurasan

I'm eating egg,

on this small space
of the kitchen table –

one bite-size piece
            cutting it
from the rest

                    yellow taste

and the whole table's a mess   go-cha go-cha, here-there
here-there:

    leftover fried smelt, tail curved in air,
        box of kleenex,
                    large pot
        of cold glutinous rice, the

    sticky bottle of *shoyu*

& this one corner,
is mine.

                    Kimurasan, an old
family friend,
writes a letter
(in Japanese)

there;

                Kimurasan,
fisherman how many years
his gillnetter, his seine-net
working the Skeena, 'Shkeena',
his *kazu-no-ko* (herring roe), B.C. sockeye,
red spring, coho, steelhead; there

on this table
his hand   the go-cha go-cha,

his bag full of thoughts, his
corner

this world.

Image

each shiny green
leaf,   silent,   plant's
unravel of damp soil.
my eyes grope
here again through night
glimmer that glimmer just
what that
before dawn
my fingers break it, dawn light
off each
green image held
shining, leaf,
    momentarily,
speech,
left.

an excerpt from the eastern white pine
language project

you come into the pines.

in the North,
you are coming into
the pines, now.

you are north
of North Bay, now
jack, red, to white pines,
it's fun picking them out.

snow, granular
like sugar;
night receding   across the lines
light, daylight and now
and you are coming into
the brittle snap

cold –

  a descent

      mouth open
the altitude and
rock face,
to the dark water,
mirror of stars.

Metapoeic

that indifference
is sinuous
: a sign.

   pigeons fly away
   at any human movement
   : a

Shield

granite rocks
the
   interior

forests'

snow,   white-out

first words
mouth   erase

kindle into
a type of brush fyre

2

the mirror

3

Spanish Dharma

this finger of night
bleeds. this city of
things to do.
here. is it where
all secret pass
-ages out of a
couple's des-
pair have left? to-
gether do we look,
and look? at her.
her cast   / old in
doorway
/ a mirror image whose
mottled teeth brown
chews, mouth open
her gums. smile.
smile, wandering breath,
into night's cor
-ner.
the dull throbs
of too many things re-
peated.

repeated in the
swing of night
singer's
voice, taint of dust,
vine and blood, stomping
feet.
such doubt
swings with night's
marked finger.

this voice:
an icicle blade
splits the spine
bolt up-
right sharp
ridge of hard
wooden chair into
my back.
icicle or crescent
moon's fragmentary
cycle in me,
its streamy fullness
a body's
returning loss.

The Dark

the dark.
separate itself   'it'
from this sound within
of thought.
the dark the dark the scratch I think
/ pencil's movement, on the page,
a spelling etched to semblant sleep
the dark; it is heard
the word this
only outline
can be, message
possibly: we know what
our own bodies contain.
        (the separation.
the
dark.   (like

paintings –
Monet brush again and a-
gain the cathedral at Rouen
over and over
to memory my memory within
of them, the paintings
the scratch deep advance
to rest in singular line
upon the train of thought.)

La danseuse

It is the way the dancer turns the figure onto the floor, the
speech of the daggered paragraph, chalk lines direct on wood.
(The movement which tends, which she has up to now fol-
lowed, to the marginal lines) the fissure of emotion, she is
pulled down. The choreograph, is mitred unto time is left vote /
the right vote, parrying to electorate, knowing the rhythm,
'syncopate' she is told, or is it that she remembers. And so,
emotion is held in this figure rehearsed, traced by her husband
onto the floor, the razor-blade ankle, 'Now?' she asks, 'Now,'
he says, conceit etymologically turns the dancer rebellious, her
own generated speech from the traceform's tense. The figure-
eight
moves unto its own still cross.

The commencement and contre-temps, and graduation
of wound.

My

My wish is not

the poem: my.

Precise. to capture, such detail, narrative,
lyric,
so precise.
my wish to easily
move my this right hand,
    the digits and

not move it,
them
at all.
loss.

Or can I simply know
such movement, hands
by their actions yes
in the cells
in brain of mine,
want the 'seeing
is believing' the know
of such science:

a judge when he decides that 'Sustained'
or 'Overruled'
to objection, cells are moving,
moving.

Moves:
I mean, look,
when I used to play football
the moves on a
pass pattern
running down, cutting
out
coming back through
my eyes to the
spiralling pass I –
used to watch this
Bobby Taylor
run those clear lines
the hints,
the fakes to the sidelines
spikes
underfoot digging into turf,
'he's got good moves'
ash.
my father

       ashes in the oak urn
   I kneel by the Hotoke-san
  juzu gently wraps my hands together

  repeat the Nembutsu of Jodo Shinshu

silken ash of incense stick falls only down.
  I cannot recollect the feeling of Spring!

So What! a Bashoesque
a rendition for bpNichol

the days pass.
each sense. all five. 5. of it.
my body combed, not

just the hair parted:
   ticks my mind.

but no way this, portals
breathing open / shut – so where?
if I cut off hands, feet, ears, penis
   tie up eyes. etcetera, slam
you know how it goes –
so what – I'll disappear – so what?
from a shimmering pool
another me up and at 'em.

among the lily pads among
the lily pads rustic, a pond, a log cabin, a what, plop, frog's

caught my ear.

A Legend, Probably

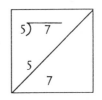

x 100 = frog

(where 7 = week)

In the Air
for Sam Johnson

there is only one cry:
all one: air

moon
sitting on your shoulder
/ your son from seed.
moon, brilliant
over snow-packed
frozen lake.
an idea at first:
the howl
eating in snow.

there is only one cry,
isn't there
in air, timber wolf
calling to moon.

there is in cold,
clear air,
the one word,
'son'
brilliant
on hard-packed snow.

Geologic

mouth granite, tongue
poplar
   which outcrop
leaf ,
heart's emblem.
compass,
topo map,
unfolds

   outc rop, contour
green, brown
distinctly
shapes the eye.

It

Directions: Take a context. Picture yourself on a café terrace, looking past the frame of an opened window, across the narrow street. There are parked cars; but they do not matter. You have a cup of espresso coffee in front of you. And across this street, it is a house which is vacant, which is partly deconstructed. Thus read:

There

there are corners of quiet
frames the sky, green
shingles of a house, a crooked
chimney

corners of quiet
at the brace of
gray concrete walls, one finds
the rivets
and screws
the brackets

there are corners
and the wood is damp
the railing broken
away when you think   intelligent(ce) corners

corners of quiet
which spell out then
the speech

tongue's motion elides
along the lips to see
that end to end
together those ties of ours
that emotion I am braced
the damn growth
against her regret bit by
bit   the not a sentence
live together

her and her image the damp
the corners of quiet
the frame of a window
of the wood,
the rivets and screws
slide it elide it
the corners of this mouth

the cool edge
this spoon and the coffee
it stirs it stirs
the street across
take a context and sip, yes,

railing, hinge.

The Blasting

what? to re
-move the whole
of it. then
more. where've I
placed it, her, him I've
this thing I'm
writing has moved,
lights flashing. the
hole of this her,
this stick of this
him. and the stream
flowing past past
this thing that I'm
writing, removing
the whole of it and
me too. excuse
me, the title.

Shining Wood

1

fingers hit rock.
fingernails forced back,
    thick with black earth,
the way of paint to
canvas – or boards nailed up,
words to paper; the slam,
black soil, hit rock,
the fingers and wrist tighten,
the pressure beneath the nails.

2

that day
that red squirrel's
crazy against
cottage porch, twitching, eating
her offerings held, that look
instant of camera's
look   just linger enough,
shutter to still: she and squirrel
but not
again   never returned again,
red squirrel that still, that shutter.
but there once

,charmed

,charmed
look,   her look.

end of April

land

(hand

which   answers for

the touch

:the breath

soil   which

words ⟷ spawn.

Gerry Shikatani
CURVD H&Z 21o
Hangnail #1o
/45, june 1983

McCaul Street

no one.
street's air, chill.

roadside piles of dried leaves
    blown, scatter noisily
over pavement:

single leaf
carried up in wind; up

I enter,

thinking,
    '... died, white
in her.'

the moon is clear in this sky,
in my small heart.

Air Poem

spice scent of after-shave
   Father wore. this room contracts.
a dime size, poem
I wrote for him, folded paper,
placed to his breast at
cremation.

Now, to write again
a new poem, freshly
   singed, this smell
in air.

Inches Grammar

the inches of my hands.

now over
thirty years.

*

What fingers
measure inches
        this palm, a line –
this phrase

utterance written,
a complete image
across which a verb
moves, inter
-cepts;

rain falls.
breath,

inches even

sky;

inches even
inches even
inches even
inches even
inches even
inches even,
now snow
turns,
    heavily
blows into
drifts.

In This and Every Place

for Rosalind; and after the work of Hamish Fulton

With each circle and with each
divide, do not eat thyself
into the red earth. Come upon,
that notion, it strikes you that motion
to cross the sand and the water.

Once I called you that cat
or maker of cats with paints and now,
I hear your far voice
oh, you are there and I am under
the column of faults, that magic
of weights and be it the earth quaking?

Do not consume thyself, cross forever,
cross forever with your voice come solvent
cross into fragrant possible.

With each circle and with each
divide I will too be there,
you will look over your shoulder;
and this too, we both know
will ache in the column
most clear and light.

(A Sparrow's Food)

damn the sweet
tweet, soft but
not dove's grey
soft, tweet
eyes, oo close
eyes sweet, peril
upon – stone's fence.
turn, crick neck

ruffled wind-blown
feathers. deep love.
of discovery and flight
deep love.   upon flower
bush, hedge, sweet's
crick neck, finding
the light love's deep
flight: heat,
burning green
desire of this quadrangle.

when reading
(*A Sparrow's*   your bend, upon
Food)   fence tasting the
autumn heat quick-flitted
concept flit.

eyes which blink
turn quick
head then flight.
meat and fish
on our tables,

death we make
and take.

Four Very Short Love Stories

for my brothers, sisters and
their families

Paris, 6 July, 1988

I

The eyes; eye. To hold a tiger s'
Tigress.

Can you smell? The fierce. Burning hands. Hands in sight, seen,
become as cross-hatched dark, which shades could say,
'*cloisonée*' uh, but abrupt 'stop.' Hands be persistent can't
shade away, hand and dark cross-hatch screen, the sliding doors
of house, all else fading to elements to God, of Wind, to God of
Thunder, in a distant place? Perspective it is, of the mountain,
the valley, all the geographies of our bodies; the deer in the val-
ley hearing its own voice – the screen sliding brings vacant to
know this voice 'mine' and I, I bite your lip my love, my sex-
partner voice, as you silently sleep only the breaths and you do
not know.

The eyes; eye. To hold a tiger s' s' s'
Tigress.
A Tail.

Who is painting history? Who is that one who paints us, as we
lie, his brush wet with distance and the wind, the S echoing
with its tail. Can you smell him, his breath? Can you smell her
teeth, the fresh wind?

2

We are walking through the maze of white chrysanthemums. I love you. You love me. Only this we say to each other. We think it's a maze – these white blooms, but truly know, or realize in time, that we trace a pattern, made in the moment we follow these pebbled and leaf-wet lanes. The discovery is gently ours. Your single breast opens wide to me, I pluck your nipple and I cannot say what rests.

These white chrysanthemums – flowers like them I've not known before. In each blossom, the centre is gold, painted with natural solution. I close my eyes and I can only see very dark green, the memory of pines. And the sky beyond is gold, painted with natural solution. You are here, little more than a flag, so small, or a kite blowing taut its string in the distant sky. I am falling asleep, riding the moist crown of your nipple. I want to return to a previous story. Your single breast tremors with lava, beneath my sandalled feet.

3

I am having fun. My brother tells me he's having fun, too. My sister yells to me, 'Yes, I'm having fun.' My oldest brother, I know, is having fun. One sister laughs and laughs. Another sister – where is she? She's spinning madly, a grin stretched over her lovely face – she can't even speak. We are six – three of us on the male side, three on the female side. One other, a brother, died many years ago, even before I was born. And my parents are sleeping and dreaming, as if all of this happened a thousand years ago, when they were Red Springs – when they were those silver-skinned salmon following the cold current of the Skeena, in B.C. We are six, I am having fun. And all of us have violet-coloured bandanas wrapped around our eyes. We are running around and around in the yard. This is entitled, 'Ancient Games Played By The Japanese in Canada.'

4

Most of all, I eat my meals with vigour, with wide-eyed plea-
sure. I touch the stove, the pan – so hot! Most, I see a time of
living in the tall grasses, blowing at the brink of the fourth hill
beyond. People are marvellous, the way they buy such extrava-
gant, wasteful clothes, so changed by fashion, so transformed
by value. My favourite wish is to live as the final inch of the tail
of a peacock shimmering in sunlight, just breaking through the
storm clouds, while the rain continues yet to fall, and the
winds, they are blowing the tall grasses in the easterly direc-
tion. Similarly, I am partial to the large tidal wave, renowned
through paintings, so clear it is in its free blue symmetry. At its
heart, which one can intercept, is a stillness, the echo of the
peacock as it catches itself in the reflection of a calm, windless
sea. I make these admissions to you sir, and ask
    that both our armies retreat,
    that we stop this fighting.
I touch the pan upon the stove, so hot!

Notes on the Text

White Pine Lodge is not, as some readers might think, a formally assembled collection of poems. It is simply, for the purposes of this current book, another process component of the *Eastern White Pine Language Project*, a research-literary work-in-progress since 1974.

White Pine Lodge is to me a mythic place where texts begin and end. White Pine Lodge is every Canadian travel brochure extolling the fabulous attractions of a vacationland lodge, a cottage resort. Remember that hokey snapshot of an angler holding the trophy-size muskie? White Pine Lodge. Remember that cornball but real gut feeling as you gazed across the lake just before sunset, the dramatic wind-blown white pine rising above other trees from the rocky outcrop shore? White Pine Lodge. Best of all, at White Pine Lodge guests are offered not only a choice of European or American Plan, but the Canadian Plan.

Half-title page: The first poem is from *Counterbomb Renga*, a collaborative performance work by poets, composers, musicians and Hiroshima and Nagasaki survivors against nuclear proliferation. It was conceived and directed by composer Udo Kasemets, performed in Toronto and broadcast on CBC Radio's *Two New Hours*. The poem is dedicated to Udo Kasemets.

Page 38: *komē*: raw rice grains.

Page 62: Phillipe Jaccottet, Swiss-French poet.

Pages 68-70: Japanese vocabulary: *Sashimi tō Maki*: raw fish and rolled (sushi). 2 *toro*: fatty belly of tuna. 3 *Nigiri*: palm-formed rice ball. 4 *Chirashi*: rice with scattered garnishes.

Page 93: Text from 'ash ...' is excerpted from my poem 'Smell of Incense in My 25th Year,' in *A Sparrow's Food*. *Hotoke-san*: Altar of risen spirit in Buddhism. *Juzu*: Buddhist rosary beads.
Nembutsu of Jodo Shinshu: recitation of faith of Buddhist sect.

The work in this collection, with a few exceptions, was written from 1980-88 and within a Canadian context. A larger body of work, set in Europe, and largely written there from 1979-87, will appear at a later date.

A bouquet to each,

Amy, Lydia, Don and especially Beverley Daurio of Aya Press.

Nelson Adams, typesetter, and Gordon Robertson, designer, at Coach House Press.

My brother Stan, whose marvellous design concepts have distinguished this and many of my previous books.

Poet, prose-writer, performance artist and occasional editor, Gerry Shikatani has been published in Canada, France, the U.S. and Japan. Born in Toronto, he continues to live there but frequently sojourns in Paris. He is also a magazine writer and broadcaster specializing in gastronomy and sports.

From the same author

The Book of Tree: a cottage journal
A Sparrow's Food (Selected Poems 1971-82)
Our Nights in Perugia
Language: voice hitting the form
Paper Doors: an anthology of Japanese-Canadian poetry
(co-editor with David Aylward)
Ship Sands Island
Haliburton
BARKING OF DOG